CONTENTS

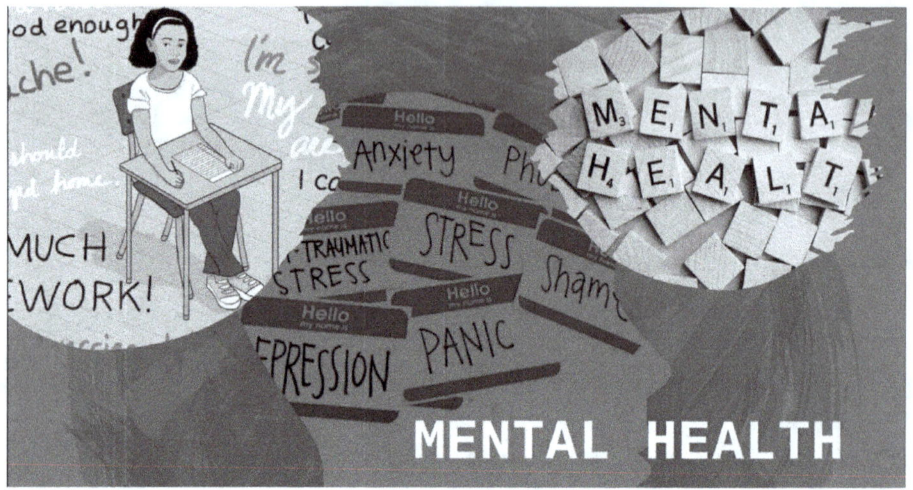

Title: "From Shadows to Light: Mastering Mental Health"

Sub-title: "Unraveling Minds: From Anxiety to Triumph - The Ultimate Guide to Mental Disorders & Celebrity Healing Journeys"

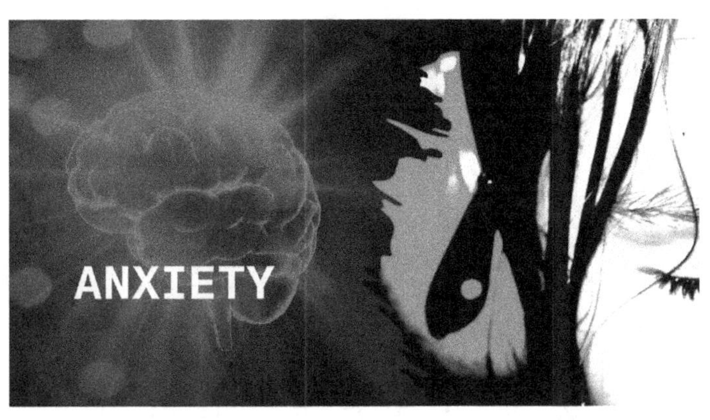

1.PSYCHOLOGICAL FACTS - 1/11 ANXIETY DISORDERS

Understanding Anxiety Disorders and Effective Solutions

Introduction

Anxiety disorders are among the most common mental health conditions, affecting a significant portion of the global population. These disorders are characterized by excessive and persistent worry, fear, and apprehension that can significantly impact a person's daily functioning and overall well-being. In this article, we will explore different types of anxiety disorders and discuss evidence-based solutions for managing and treating them effectively.

Anxiety disorders are a widespread issue, considered to be some of the most prevalent mental health conditions around the world. These conditions are hallmarked by an overwhelming sense of fear, worry, and unease, a persistent apprehension that significantly influences the way a person leads their life, affecting their daily functioning to a considerable degree.

Diverse in their nature, anxiety disorders encompass various types under their umbrella, each with unique manifestations and implications. Alongside exploring these different types, this article will also delve into the science-backed methodologies proven to manage and successfully treat anxiety disorders, providing a comprehensive overview for a better understanding of this crucial subject.

Types of Anxiety Disorders:

1. Generalized Anxiety Disorder (GAD): Individuals with GAD experience chronic and excessive worry about various aspects of

life, including work, health, and relationships.

2. Panic Disorder: Panic attacks, characterized by intense fear and physical symptoms such as heart palpitations and shortness of breath, are the hallmark of panic disorder.

3. Social Anxiety Disorder (SAD): SAD involves an intense fear of social situations and a persistent concern about being judged or embarrassed by others.

4. Specific Phobias: This type of anxiety disorder involves an intense and irrational fear of specific objects or situations, such as heights, spiders, or flying.

5. Obsessive-Compulsive Disorder (OCD): OCD is characterized by intrusive and distressing thoughts (obsessions) and repetitive behaviors or mental rituals (compulsions) aimed at reducing anxiety.

Effective Solutions for Anxiety Disorders:

1. Cognitive Behavioral Therapy (CBT): CBT is a widely recommended therapeutic approach for anxiety disorders. It helps individuals identify and challenge negative thought patterns and develop effective coping strategies. Research has shown CBT to be effective in reducing anxiety symptoms (Hofmann et al., 2012).

2. Medication: In some cases, medication may be prescribed to manage anxiety symptoms. Selective serotonin reuptake inhibitors (SSRIs) and benzodiazepines are commonly used medications, but they should be prescribed and monitored by a qualified healthcare professional.

3. Mindfulness-Based Interventions: Techniques like mindfulness meditation and relaxation exercises can help individuals with anxiety disorders develop a greater sense of calmness and improve their ability to manage anxious thoughts and physical sensations (Hoge et al., 2013).

4. Exercise and Physical Activity: Engaging in regular physical

exercise has been shown to reduce anxiety symptoms by increasing the production of endorphins, improving sleep quality, and providing a distraction from anxious thoughts (Asmundson et al., 2013).

5. Lifestyle Modifications: Adopting a healthy lifestyle that includes a balanced diet, sufficient sleep, and stress management techniques can significantly contribute to anxiety management.

6. Support Networks: Building a strong support system with friends, family, or support groups can provide emotional support and understanding, reducing feelings of isolation and anxiety.

Effective Solutions for Managing and Treating Anxiety Disorders:

Once diagnosed, several evidence-based therapeutic approaches can help manage and treat anxiety disorders effectively. These include psychotherapy, pharmacological treatments, and self-care strategies.

Psychotherapy, specifically cognitive-behavioral therapy (CBT), has proven highly effective against most types of anxiety disorders. CBT enables individuals to identify and challenge their thought patterns and behaviors that trigger and sustain anxiety, thereby teaching them to respond to anxiety-provoking situations more effectively.

Pharmacological treatments can also play an essential role in treating anxiety disorders. Antidepressants, benzodiazepines, and beta-blockers are among the commonly prescribed medications that help reduce the symptoms of anxiety.

Lastly, adopting a healthy lifestyle can complement these treatments. Regular exercise, a balanced diet, adequate sleep, mindful practices like yoga and meditation, and limiting caffeine and alcohol consumption can collectively help manage anxiety levels.

Additionally, support from close-knit relationships (family and friends) and self-help groups can provide significant relief, offering a space to share experiences and learn how others cope with their anxiety.

In conclusion, understanding the nature and types of anxiety disorders, along with their effective management strategies, is critical for addressing this widespread mental health condition. As science continues to progress, the hope is to provide even better methods to help individuals combat and manage their anxiety disorders in the future.

Anxiety disorders can significantly impact an individual's quality of life, but effective solutions are available. A combination of evidence-based treatments, such as cognitive-behavioral therapy, medication, mindfulness-based interventions, and lifestyle modifications, can help individuals manage and overcome anxiety symptoms. It is important to consult with mental health professionals to determine the most appropriate treatment plan for each individual.

References:
- Hofmann, S. G., et al. (2012). The efficacy of cognitive behavioral therapy: A review of meta-analyses. Cognitive Therapy and Research, 36(5), 427-440.
- Hoge, E. A., et al. (2013). The effect of mindfulness meditation training on biological acute stress responses in generalized anxiety disorder. Psychiatry Research, 210(3), 1031-1038.
- Asmundson, G. J., et al. (2013). Exercise for mood and anxiety disorders: A review of empirical evidence. Journal of Affective Disorders, 151(2), 722-731.

2.PSYCHOLOGICAL FACTS 2/11 - DEPRESSION & SOLUTIONS

Understanding Depression and Effective Solutions

Introduction

Depression is an increasingly prevalent yet frequently misunderstood mental health condition. It brings a substantial burden, not only affecting an individual's mental and emotional state but also impacting their physical health and overall quality of life. This condition typically manifests as a pervasive sense of sadness, a feeling of despair, or a consistent loss of interest in previously enjoyed activities.

On top of these emotional symptoms, those experiencing depression can also deal with a variety of cognitive and somatic symptoms. These may include concentration challenges, extreme fatigue, sleep disturbances, and changes in appetite. The severity and duration of these symptoms can vary greatly but, in general, they persist for two weeks or more. In today's discussion, we will delve deeper into the nature of depression, its various types, and evidence-based solutions for its effective management and treatment.

Understanding Depression:

Depression, also known as major depressive disorder or clinical depression, is far more complex than temporary emotional responses to life challenges. It is a serious mental health condition that demands attention, understanding, and appropriate treatment.

Understanding the different forms of depression is essential as treatment can vary based on the specific type diagnosed. Major

Depressive Disorder (MDD), Persistent Depressive Disorder (PDD), Bipolar Disorder, Postpartum Depression, and Seasonal Affective Disorder (SAD) are some of the common forms that can be observed. The unique characteristics of each type can significantly affect an individual's experiences and treatment requirements.

Evidence-based Solutions for Managing and Treating Depression:

Holistic management of depression involves a blend of numerous interventions. Depending on the severity, duration, and type of depression, a combination of psychotherapy, medication, lifestyle changes, and supportive measures may be required.

Psychotherapy forms the core of many depression management strategies. Cognitive Behavioral Therapy (CBT), Interpersonal Therapy (IPT), and Psychodynamic Therapy are among the most effective therapeutic approaches. They work by helping individuals identify harmful thought patterns and teaching strategies to manage and overcome them.

Medication, such as selective serotonin reuptake inhibitors (SSRIs) and atypical antidepressants, can also play a crucial role in treating depression by aiding in rebalancing brain chemicals associated with mood regulation. These medications, when administered appropriately, can significantly improve depressive symptoms.

Lifestyle modifications such as regular exercise, a well-balanced diet, adequate sleep, and avoiding alcohol and drugs have also proven to be beneficial in managing symptoms and improving overall well-being.

Additionally, social support from friends, family, and support groups can provide emotional comfort and practical assistance. Mindfulness-based interventions, including yoga, meditation, and mindfulness-based cognitive therapy (MBCT), can also foster resilience and alleviate depressive symptoms.

Recently, innovative options like Transcranial Magnetic Stimulation (TMS) have emerged as potential solutions for treatment-resistant depression. These advanced techniques offer hope for those who haven't responded sufficiently to conventional treatments.

Types of Depression:

1. Major Depressive Disorder (MDD): MDD involves persistent feelings of sadness, hopelessness, and a loss of interest in activities that were once enjoyable.

2. Persistent Depressive Disorder (PDD): PDD, also known as dysthymia, is characterized by a chronic but less severe form of depression lasting for at least two years.

3. Postpartum Depression: Experienced by some women after childbirth, postpartum depression involves intense feelings of sadness, anxiety, and exhaustion that can interfere with daily functioning.

4. Seasonal Affective Disorder (SAD): SAD is a subtype of depression that occurs during specific seasons, typically during winter when there is reduced exposure to sunlight.

Effective Solutions for Depression:

1. Psychotherapy: Different forms of psychotherapy, such as Cognitive Behavioral Therapy (CBT) and Interpersonal Therapy (IPT), have shown effectiveness in treating depression by helping individuals identify negative thought patterns, develop coping strategies, and improve interpersonal relationships (Cuijpers et al., 2013).

2. Medication: Antidepressant medications, such as selective serotonin reuptake inhibitors (SSRIs) and serotonin-norepinephrine reuptake inhibitors (SNRIs), are commonly prescribed to alleviate symptoms of depression. Medication

should be prescribed and monitored by a qualified healthcare professional.

3. Lifestyle Modifications: Engaging in regular physical exercise, maintaining a healthy diet, ensuring adequate sleep, and reducing stress can significantly contribute to managing depression symptoms (Schuch et al., 2021).

4. Social Support: Building and maintaining strong social connections can provide emotional support and reduce feelings of isolation. Participating in support groups or seeking help from friends and family members can be valuable (Teo et al., 2018).

5. Mindfulness-Based Interventions: Techniques like mindfulness meditation and yoga have shown promise in reducing depression symptoms by increasing self-awareness, promoting relaxation, and improving emotional regulation (Khoury et al., 2013).

6. Transcranial Magnetic Stimulation (TMS): TMS is a non-invasive procedure that uses magnetic fields to stimulate specific areas of the brain. It has been approved as a treatment for depression, particularly for individuals who have not responded to other interventions (McClintock et al., 2018).

Conclusion:

Depression is a complex mental health condition that can significantly impact an individual's well-being. Effective solutions for managing and treating depression include psychotherapy, medication, lifestyle modifications, social support, mindfulness-based interventions, and innovative techniques like TMS. It is important to consult with mental health professionals to determine the most appropriate treatment plan for each individual.

Depression is a challenging mental health condition that poses significant harm to an individual's health, productivity, and overall well-being. The combination of understanding its complexities, acknowledging the various types, and applying evidence-based solutions are crucial for managing and effectively treating this condition.

However, due to the highly individual nature of depression, it is always recommended to consult with mental health professionals. They can provide personalized assessment and treatments, ensuring a care plan tailored to the needs and circumstances of each person.

References:
- Cuijpers, P., et al. (2013). Psychotherapy for depression in adults: A meta-analysis of comparative outcome studies. Journal of Consulting and Clinical Psychology, 81(3), 531-543.
- Schuch, F. B., et al. (2021). Exercise as a treatment for depression: A meta-analysis adjusting for publication bias. Journal of Psychiatric Research, 134, 129-139.
- Teo, A. R., et al. (2018). Social isolation associated with depression: A case report of hikikomori. International Journal of Social Psychiatry, 64(5), 488-491.
- Khoury, B., et al. (2013). Mindfulness-based stress reduction for healthy individuals: A meta-analysis. Journal of Psychosomatic Research, 78(6), 519-528.
- McClintock, S. M., et al. (2018). Consensus recommendations for the clinical application of repetitive transcranial magnetic stimulation (rTMS) in the treatment of depression. Journal of Clinical Psychiatry, 79(1).

3. PSYCHOLOGICAL FACTS 3-11 - UNDERSTANDING POST-TRAUMATIC STRESS (PTSD)

Understanding Post-Traumatic Stress Disorder (PTSD): Symptoms and Treatment

Introduction

Post-Traumatic Stress Disorder (PTSD) is a mental health condition that can develop after experiencing or witnessing a traumatic event. It is characterized by a range of symptoms that can significantly impact an individual's daily life. In this article, we will explore the symptoms of PTSD, its effects, and evidence-based treatments for effectively managing and treating this disorder.

Symptoms of PTSD:

1. Intrusive Thoughts: Recurrent and distressing memories, nightmares, or flashbacks related to the traumatic event.

2. Avoidance: Avoiding triggers or reminders of the trauma, including people, places, or activities associated with the traumatic event.

3. Negative Mood and Cognition: Persistent negative emotions, distorted thoughts about oneself or the world, feelings of detachment, or an inability to experience positive emotions.

4. Hyperarousal: Heightened startle response, difficulty sleeping, irritability, and hypervigilance.

5. Emotional Reactivity: Experiencing intense emotional reactions, including anger, guilt, shame, or fear, often disproportionate to the current situation.

Effective Treatments for PTSD:

1.   Trauma-Focused Psychotherapy: Various psychotherapy approaches have been shown to be effective in treating PTSD, including Cognitive Processing Therapy (CPT) and Prolonged Exposure (PE) therapy. These therapies help individuals process and reframe traumatic memories, challenge negative beliefs, and develop healthy coping mechanisms (Bisson et al., 2013).

2. Eye Movement Desensitization and Reprocessing (EMDR): EMDR is a specialized therapy that incorporates eye movements or other forms of bilateral stimulation to facilitate the processing of traumatic memories and reduce associated distress (Cusack et al., 2016).

3. Medication: Selective serotonin reuptake inhibitors (SSRIs), such as sertraline and paroxetine, are commonly prescribed to alleviate symptoms of PTSD. Medication should be prescribed and monitored by a qualified healthcare professional.

4. Cognitive-Behavioral Therapies (CBTs): CBT approaches, such as Cognitive Restructuring and Stress Inoculation Training (SIT), can help individuals identify and challenge negative thinking patterns and develop effective coping strategies for managing PTSD symptoms (Ehlers et al., 2005).

5. Group Therapy and Peer Support: Participating in group therapy or support groups with individuals who have experienced similar traumas can provide validation, understanding, and a sense of belonging, reducing feelings of isolation (Resick et al., 2008).

6. Self-Care and Stress Management: Engaging in activities that promote self-care, such as exercise, relaxation techniques, and maintaining a healthy lifestyle, can contribute to overall well-being and symptom management.

Post-Traumatic Stress Disorder (PTSD) typically emerges subsequent to an individual being exposed to a distressing or life-threatening event. This could include experiences such as severe accidents, physical or sexual assault, combat, disasters, or witnessing a death. For some individuals, the traumatic event may immediately precipitate symptoms of PTSD, while for others, these indications may surface weeks, months, or even years after the event.

Symptoms of PTSD can be broadly categorized into four main types: Intrusive memories of the trauma, negative thinking and mood alterations, changes in physical and emotional reactions, and avoidance. Recurrent, intrusive, and distressing recollections of the traumatic event can cause significant disruption to a person's waking cycle and may also adversely impact their sleep with nightmares. Concurrently, they may intentionally or subconsciously avoid situations that could serve as potential reminders of the traumatic event.

Moreover, affected individuals often experience alterations in mood and cognition, such as feelings of detachment from others, pervasive negative emotional states, feelings of guilt, and diminished interest in previously enjoyed activities. Changes might also occur in emotional and physical reactions, including hypervigilance, pronounced startle response, difficulty sleeping, issues with concentration, or self-destructive behavior.

The effects of PTSD can be pervasive and can extend into most, if not all, areas of an individual's life. Work performance may suffer, relationships can be strained, and, in some cases, the individual may resort to substance abuse as a maladaptive coping mechanism. It is not uncommon for individuals experiencing PTSD to circularly struggle with comorbid mental health issues such as depression, anxiety, and other mood or substance use disorders.

As daunting as the symptoms of PTSD may seem, there's a silver lining - numerous evidence-based treatments exist that have proven remarkably effective in managing and treating this disorder. One of the most common approaches for treating PTSD is trauma-focused cognitive-behavioral therapy (CBT). CBT involves identifying and restructuring negative thought patterns that perpetuate symptoms of PTSD.

Another established treatment method is Eye Movement Desensitization and Reprocessing (EMDR). EMDR proactively uses bilateral stimulation, such as eye movements, to help individuals process and make sense of their traumatic memories.

Medication, including selective serotonin reuptake inhibitors (SSRIs) and serotonin and norepinephrine reuptake inhibitors (SNRIs), are also regularly used to help alleviate symptoms of PTSD. These, combined with psychotherapy, often significantly benefit those who have PTSD.

Group therapy provides a therapeutic space where affected individuals can share their experiences and coping strategies with others who are enduring similar struggles, contributing to a sense of understanding and companionship throughout recovery.

Including self-care practices in the treatment plan is equally important, encompassing a well-balanced diet, regular physical exercise, sufficient sleep, mindfulness exercises, and supportive social interactions to promote overall wellness and resilience.

Conclusion:

Post-Traumatic Stress Disorder (PTSD) is a complex mental health condition elicited by witnessing or experiencing traumatic events. It culminates in a multitude of symptoms capable of permeating multiple aspects of a person's life. However, the presence of evidence-based treatments such as trauma-focused psychotherapy, EMDR, medications, CBT, group therapy, and self-care practices empower individuals to effectively combat this disorder.

It is of utmost importance for individuals presenting symptoms of PTSD to reach out for professional help. In doing so, they can receive a comprehensive diagnosis integrating the specifics of their unique experience, and engage in a customized treatment plan designed to their needs.

While PTSD indeed presents pronounced challenges, there's an undeniable strength in seeking help, a testament to the resilience of the human spirit, heralding the hopeful start of a healing process.

References:
- Bisson, J. I., et al. (2013). Psychological treatments for chronic post-traumatic stress disorder: Systematic review and meta-analysis. British Journal of Psychiatry, 202(2), 97-104.
- Cusack, K., et al. (2016). Psychological treatments for post-traumatic stress disorder in adults: A systematic review and meta-analysis of randomized controlled trials. Clinical Psychology Review, 43, 128-141.
- Ehlers, A., et al. (2005). Cognitive therapy for post-traumatic stress disorder: Development and evaluation. Behaviour Research and Therapy, 43(4), 413-431.
- Resick, P. A., et al. (2008). Group treatment of posttraumatic stress disorder: A feasibility study. Journal of Traumatic Stress, 21(2), 209-216.

4.PSYCHOLOGICAL FACTS 4-11 - ATTENTION DEFICIT HYPERACTIVITY DISORDER (ADHD)

ADHD Decoded: Unlocking the Mystery of the Hyperactive Mind

Introduction

Attention Deficit Hyperactivity Disorder (ADHD) is a neurodevelopmental disorder that commonly begins in childhood and can persist into adulthood. It is characterized by persistent patterns of inattention, hyperactivity, and impulsivity that can significantly impact an individual's daily functioning and quality of life. In this article, we will explore the symptoms of ADHD, its effects, and evidence-based strategies for effectively managing and treating this disorder.

Attention Deficit Hyperactivity Disorder, short for ADHD, is a neurodevelopmental disorder often diagnosed in childhood and potentially continuing into adulthood. This condition expresses itself through a persistent pattern of inattention, hyperactivity, and impulsivity. These patterns can gravely influence an individual's capacity to operate daily and can significantly lessen the quality of their life.

Although ADHD is primarily diagnosed in children, it is not exclusive to this age group as it can also pervade the lives of adults. In this comprehensive perspective, we aim to examine the symptoms of ADHD, its consequences on the psychological and emotional aspects of individuals' lives wholeheartedly, and elucidate established, scientifically-backed strategies for effectively managing and treating this disorder.

Defining more precisely, ADHD is a persistent neurobiological disorder identified by persistent patterns of hyperactivity, impulsivity, and attention difficulty. While these symptoms are generally considered normal qualities expressed by nearly all children, the intensity and frequency of these behaviors in children and individuals with ADHD far exceed those in the general population, causing substantial impairment in various aspects of life.

Defining Symptoms

ADHD symptoms manifest in a wide range of behaviors and have a substantial impact on people's well-being. A few of the common symptoms include trouble focusing on tasks, overactivity, difficulties adhering to instructions, easy distraction, disinclination in participating in tasks requiring thoughtfulness and focus, impatience, and leaving tasks unfinished.

The severity and combination of symptoms may significantly vary from one person to another depending on their environment and genetic make-up.

Symptoms of ADHD

1. Inattention: Difficulty sustaining attention, easily distracted, making careless mistakes, struggling with organization and planning.

2. Hyperactivity: Restlessness, excessive talking, difficulty staying seated, fidgeting, and difficulty engaging in quiet activities.

3. Impulsivity: Acting without thinking, interrupting others, difficulty waiting for turns, and engaging in risky behaviors.

Management and Treatment of ADHD

1. Behavioral Therapy: Behavioral interventions, such as Parent Training and Classroom Management, can help individuals with ADHD develop and reinforce appropriate behaviors, improve self-control, and enhance organizational skills (Sonuga-Barke et al., 2013).

2. Medication: Stimulant medications, such as methylphenidate and amphetamines, are commonly prescribed to manage ADHD symptoms. Non-stimulant medications like atomoxetine may also be used. Medication should be prescribed and monitored by a qualified healthcare professional.

3. Cognitive-Behavioral Therapy (CBT): CBT interventions for ADHD aim to improve executive functioning skills, enhance self-regulation, and address emotional and social difficulties. It can be beneficial for individuals with ADHD, particularly when combined with medication (Safren et al., 2005).

4. Educational Support and Accommodations: Providing academic support, such as individualized education plans (IEPs) or Section 504 plans, can help individuals with ADHD succeed in educational settings. This may include extended time for assignments, preferential seating, or additional support from teachers.

5. Parent and Teacher Training: Educating parents and teachers about ADHD, its symptoms, and strategies for managing behaviors can improve communication, consistency, and understanding.

Parent and teacher training programs have been shown to be effective in reducing ADHD-related impairments (Evans et al., 2018).

6. Supportive Environment: Creating a supportive and structured environment can help individuals with ADHD manage their symptoms. This includes clear routines, breaking tasks into manageable steps, and providing positive reinforcement for desired behaviors.

ADHD often carries a substantial burden for those living with the condition. The condition can lead to struggles in academics, strained relationships, and difficulties with self-esteem. Moreover, there is an increase in the risk of injuries and substance misuse associated with individuals diagnosed with ADHD. The financial burden imposed by this condition through medical costs and loss of productivity also adds to the adversity faced by the affected individuals and families.

Evidence-Based Strategies for Management and Treatment

Effective management of ADHD requires a multidimensional approach. Behavioral therapy, personalized educational support, and appropriate medication are typically part of the regimen. Behavioral intervention involves specific techniques to alter behavior positively, often requiring participation from parents, teachers, and other significant figures in the child's life.

Medication, such as stimulants and non-stimulants, help manage symptoms by altering the brain chemistry to improve concentration and control impulses. Personalized educational support aims to provide assistance and accommodations in the academic setting, making it easier for the individuals with ADHD to perform better.

Creating a supportive environment is vital to the well-being of those with ADHD. Coping mechanisms and organizational tools can help individuals manage everyday tasks, and a supportive community can significantly promote psychological well-being.

Attention Deficit Hyperactivity Disorder (ADHD) is a neurodevelopmental disorder affecting people across all age groups. The effective management of ADHD typically necessitates a combination of behavioral therapy, medication, custom educational support, and a supportive environment.

For individuals diagnosed with this disorder, it is paramount to maintain active involvement with healthcare providers, educators, and their supportive community to devise personalized strategies for managing symptoms. The ultimate goal is to optimize their overall well-being, productivity level, and ability to enjoy a high quality of life. ADHD is a lifelong journey, but with proper understanding and the right management techniques, it is certainly a journey that can be navigated successfully.

Conclusion:

Attention Deficit Hyperactivity Disorder (ADHD) is a neurodevelopmental disorder that affects individuals of all ages. Effective management of ADHD involves a combination of behavioral therapy, medication, educational support, and creating a supportive environment. It is important for individuals with ADHD to work closely with healthcare professionals, educators, and support networks to develop personalized strategies for managing symptoms and optimizing their overall well-being.

References:
- Sonuga-Barke, E. J., et al. (2013). Nonpharmacological interventions for ADHD: systematic review and meta-analyses of randomized controlled trials of dietary and psychological treatments.

American Journal of Psychiatry, 170(3), 275-289.
- Safren, S. A., et al. (2005). Cognitive-behavioral therapy for ADHD in medication-treated adults

with continued symptoms. Behaviour Research and Therapy, 43(7), 831-842.
- Evans, S. W., et al. (2018). Systematic review of school-based interventions for students with attention-deficit/hyperactivity disorder. School Mental Health, 10(2), 99-120.

5. PSYCHOLOGICAL FACTS 5-11 – UNDERSTANDING SUBSTANCE ABUSE DISORDERS

Understanding Substance Abuse Disorders: Causes, Effects, and Treatment

Introduction

Substance abuse disorders, a category of conditions that are as complex as they are persistent, are characterized by an overwhelming compulsive urge to persistently use various substances, often in harmful quantities, regardless of the ensuing negative impacts. The nature of these disorders lies in the inherent inability of the affected individuals to control their substance use, creating a recurring cycle of harm and misuse.

These behavioral disorders can have considerable, life-altering effects, extensively influencing an individual's physical health, mental stability, interpersonal relationships, and their overall quality of life. They often result in self-destructive behaviors that not only affect the individual but also create ripple effects in their circle of relationships, from immediate family to communities, underlining its intense and far-reaching implications.

In the upcoming sections of the article, we will delve deeper and scrutinize the multifaceted causes of substance abuse disorders. We aim to shed light on the blend of biological, psychological, and sociocultural factors that contribute to the initial substance use and the transition from use to misuse, facilitating a comprehensive understanding of the root causes of these disorders.

Moreover, we will explore the wide array of effects substance abuse disorders can have on individuals and surrounding communities. You will find an examination of the apparent physical health detriments, as well as the crucial mental health implications and the insidious social ramifications they spur.

Finally, we will examine a spectrum of evidence-based treatment approaches for substance abuse disorders, highlighting the various methodologies in use today. By evaluating psychotherapeutic methods, pharmacological interventions, and community-based approaches, we will provide a holistic portrayal of the therapeutic landscape for these disorders, including the strengths and weaknesses of different treatments.

In this way, we endeavor to provide you with an encompassing perspective on substance abuse disorders: from their causes and effects to existing therapeutic interventions, in hope of empowering readers with knowledge to better comprehend these complex disorders.

Causes of Substance Abuse Disorders

1. Genetic Factors: Research suggests that genetic factors contribute to an individual's susceptibility to substance abuse disorders. Certain genes may influence an individual's response to substances and their risk of developing addiction (Volkow et al., 2016).

2. Environmental Factors: Factors such as peer influence, exposure to substance use, early initiation of drug use, and a history of trauma or abuse can increase the likelihood of developing a substance abuse disorder (National Institute on Drug Abuse, 2020).

3. Co-occurring Mental Health Disorders: Substance abuse disorders often co-occur with mental health conditions, such as depression, anxiety, or trauma-related disorders. Individuals may turn to substances as a way to self-medicate or alleviate symptoms.

Effects of Substance Abuse Disorders

1. Physical Health Consequences: Substance abuse can lead to various health issues, including liver damage, cardiovascular problems, respiratory disorders, and an increased risk of infectious diseases (World Health Organization, 2018).

2. Mental Health Implications: Substance abuse disorders are associated with an elevated risk of developing mental health disorders such as depression, anxiety, psychosis, and cognitive impairments (Hasin et al., 2016).

3. Impaired Relationships and Social Functioning: Substance abuse can strain relationships with family, friends, and colleagues. It may lead to isolation, conflicts, and difficulties fulfilling personal and professional responsibilities.

Treatment of Substance Abuse Disorders

1. Detoxification: Medically supervised detoxification helps individuals safely manage withdrawal symptoms and overcome physical dependence on substances.

2. Behavioral Therapies: Evidence-based behavioral therapies, such as Cognitive Behavioral Therapy (CBT), Motivational Interviewing (MI), and Contingency Management (CM), can help individuals develop coping skills, address underlying issues, and modify unhealthy behaviors (National Institute on Drug Abuse, 2018).

3. Medication-Assisted Treatment (MAT): Medications, such as methadone, buprenorphine, and naltrexone, can be used as part of a comprehensive treatment plan for opioid or alcohol addiction. These medications help reduce cravings, manage withdrawal symptoms, and support long-term recovery.

4. Support Groups and Peer Support: Participating in support groups, such as 12-Step programs (e.g., Alcoholics Anonymous, Narcotics Anonymous), can provide individuals with a sense of

community, encouragement, and accountability.

5. Holistic Approaches: Integrating holistic practices, such as mindfulness meditation, yoga, exercise, and art therapy, can complement traditional treatment approaches and promote overall well-being.

Conclusion

Substance abuse disorders, undeniably intricate and multifaceted in nature, generate far-reaching and damaging consequences not only on the person suffering directly but also on their loved ones, and society at large.

The destructive cynosure of these disorders lies in their ability to deteriorate several aspects of an individual's life - their physical and mental health, interpersonal relationships, and all-inclusive functioning, leading to a reduced quality of life and potential hindrances in personal development.

Moreover, these disorders stretch beyond inflicting immediate harm and may cause ripple effects that attribute to long-term physiological complications, emotionally draining experiences, and relationship strains.

They can dismantle relationships, disrupt careers, and contribute to substantial societal concerns such as public health and safety issues, adding a layer of complexity to their management and understanding.

When it comes to effective treatment for these overwhelming disorders, there's no 'one-size-fits-all'. Effectual intervention requires a diverse, comprehensive, and integrated approach that accounts for the unique circumstances of each individual's condition. This approach may consist of, but is not limited to, the initial detoxification processes - an essential step aimed at physical stabilization, followed by an all-embracing range of evidence-based behavioral therapies that target the cognitive and emotional aspects of substance abuse.

Medication-assisted treatments play a crucial role in supplementing this recovery journey, working to minimize withdrawal symptoms, curb cravings, and address any co-occurring mental health conditions, thereby providing a well-rounded, scientifically-proven approach to tackling these conditions.

Additionally, support from community-based groups, peers, and professional counselors during this rigorous journey often serves as a catalyst, accelerating the transition from a state of substance dependency to a more hopeful and stable life. Fostering a sense of belonging, these groups harness the power of shared experiences, providing both moral and practical support to those grappling with recovery.

Beyond this, exploring holistic interventions such as mind-body therapies, nutritional guidance, and lifestyle changes, pave the way for a more thorough and personalized healing process. These interventions underline the necessity of nurturing both physical and mental health, contributing to overall well-being and fostering resilience in the face of setbacks.

Hence, it is of utmost importance for individuals wrestling with substance abuse disorders to seek and welcome professional assistance. Engaging actively in a personalized and adaptive treatment plan tailored to individual needs and conditions is paramount in achieving long-lasting sobriety and recovery, effectively paving the way towards a healthier life and a brighter future. Life with substance abuse disorders is challenging, but remember, recovery is not just possible, it's a path to a revitalized existence.

References:
- Volkow, N. D., et al. (2016). Genetics and the brain circuitry of addiction. New England Journal of Medicine, 374(4), 363-371.
- National Institute on Drug Abuse. (2020). DrugFacts: Understanding Drug Use and Addiction.

- World Health Organization. (2018). Substance abuse.
- Hasin, D. S., et al. (2016). Epidemiology of adult DSM-5 major depressive disorder and its specifiers in the United States. JAMA Psychiatry, 73(4), 336-346.
- National Institute on Drug Abuse. (2018). Principles of Drug Addiction Treatment: A Research-Based Guide – Third Edition.

31

6. PSYCHOLOGICAL FACTS 6-11 - UNDERSTANDING EATING DISORDER

Understanding Eating Disorders: Causes, Effects, andEffective Treatment Approaches

Introduction

Eating disorders, a term encompassing a range of complex mental health conditions, are typified by abnormal eating habits and an excessive focus on body weight, shape, and diet. These disorders, when left unchecked, can lead to dire physical and mental health repercussions. They not only disrupt a person's nourishment intake but also their perception of self, spiraling often into an obsession with their body's appearance and their diet.

These conditions, underpinned by multifaceted psychological mechanisms, are far more than just 'about food'. They represent deeper complexities, predominantly rooted in cognitive and emotional health, illustrating disturbing correlations between the mind and the body. The causes are manifold, and they often involve a combination of genetic, biological, behavioural, psychological, and sociocultural factors. Untangling these origins is a crucial part of understanding eating disorders and establishes a fundamental premise for our discussion.

The impacts of these disorders are profoundly damaging, varying in effects. On the physical front, eating disorders can lead to profound health issues encompassing every vital organ system in our body. The psychological aftermath is just as detrimental, provoking significant distress and impaired functioning, often manifesting further mental health problems such as anxiety, depression, or obsessive-compulsive disorder.

In this comprehensive review, we will delve deeper into the world of eating disorders, endeavouring to gain a layered understanding of their causes and effects. More importantly, we will sift through scientific evidence to identify effective treatment approaches. These treatments, based on empirical evidence and clinical expertise, often involve a blend of psychological therapy, nutritional education, medical monitoring and, sometimes, medication.

By sharing this knowledge, our ultimate goal is to contribute to a more informed dialogue on the issue — promoting early detection, encouraging timely treatment and supporting those who live with these disorders to regain control over their lives. As we shine a light on these misunderstood and often stigmatized conditions, our hope is that this article demystifies misconceptions, fosters empathy, and inspires action.

Causes of Eating Disorders

1. Genetic Factors: Research suggests a genetic predisposition to eating disorders, with certain genes contributing to an individual's susceptibility (Bulik et al., 2016).

2. Psychological Factors: Psychological factors, such as low self-esteem, perfectionism, body dissatisfaction, and distorted body image, play a significant role in the development of eating disorders.

3. Environmental Influences: Societal pressures, cultural ideals of beauty, and exposure to negative body images in media can contribute to the development of eating disorders (Stice, 2002).

Effects of Eating Disorders

1. Physical Health Consequences: Eating disorders can lead to severe medical complications, including malnutrition, electrolyte imbalances, organ damage, osteoporosis, and hormonal disruptions (National Eating Disorders Association, 2021).

2. Psychological and Emotional Impact: Eating disorders are associated with increased rates of depression, anxiety, obsessive-compulsive disorder, self-harm, and suicidal ideation (Arcelus et al., 2011).

3. Social and Interpersonal Difficulties: Eating disorders can strain relationships, isolation, and impair social functioning, leading to reduced quality of life and hindered personal and professional growth.

Effective Treatment Approaches for Eating Disorders

1. Psychotherapy: Psychotherapy, such as Cognitive Behavioral Therapy (CBT), is a widely recognized and effective treatment approach for eating disorders. It helps individuals identify and challenge distorted thoughts and behaviors, develop healthy coping mechanisms, and improve body image (Fairburn et al., 2015).

2. Family-Based Treatment (FBT): FBT, also known as the Maudsley approach, is particularly effective for adolescents with eating disorders. It involves the active involvement of the family in the treatment process, focusing on restoring weight, normalizing eating behaviors, and addressing family dynamics (Lock et al., 2010).

3. Medical and Nutritional Management: In severe cases, medical stabilization and nutritional rehabilitation may be necessary. This involves close monitoring of physical health, addressing nutritional deficiencies, and providing guidance on healthy eating patterns.

4. Support Groups and Peer Support: Participating in support groups, such as Eating Disorders Anonymous or group therapy, can provide individuals with a sense of community, understanding, and encouragement during recovery.

5. Medication: Medication may be prescribed as an adjunct to

psychotherapy for individuals with co-occurring mental health conditions, such as depression or anxiety. However, medication alone is not considered a primary treatment for eating disorders.

Conclusion

Eating disorders, representing a spectrum of complex conditions, are intricate psychological entanglements that strike at the heart of a person's physical and mental wellness. They manifest themselves in myriad ways, leaving behind an extensive trail of physical and emotional damage.

Fighting these disorders requires deploying various strategies, forming a multi-pronged approach that is both comprehensive and individualized.

Effective interventions for eating disorders are underlined by the inclusion of psychotherapy, a crucial component that aids in understanding and reshaping harmful thought patterns. The utilization of various therapeutic modalities–individual, group, or family-focused–can be instrumental in encompassing all angles of recovery, thereby addressing the underlying issues and working towards reinstituting a healthy relationship with food and body.

Adding another dimension are family involvements and support groups. These play a pivotal role in deconstructing stigma, encouraging open conversation about the illness, and providing the much-needed emotional backing. The experiential sharing and collective strength derived from these groups are invaluable in the healing process.

Equally as crucial is medical and nutritional management conducted by skilled healthcare professionals. This component recognizes the physiological toll of eating disorders and aims to restore the body to a state of balanced nutrition. Individualized dietary plans, consistent monitoring, and a gradual shift towards independent meal planning and preparation are essential steps towards sensible nutritional habits.

In some instances, medication might also be considered a viable part of the treatment equation. Administered under the watchful eye of a professional, these can help manage co-existing mental health issues like depression or anxiety that often accompany eating disorders.

Lastly, it is of paramount importance for individuals suffering from eating disorders to actively seek professional help and willingly engage in customized recovery strategies. This commitment to a comprehensive treatment plan is a significant stride towards lasting recovery, improved overall well-being, and the reclaiming of one's life in its entirety.

Moreover, it is crucial to remember that the path to recovery is rarely linear. It demands patience, perseverance, and unwavering support. Awareness, early intervention, and an uncompromising commitment to recovery are ultimately key to navigating the complexities of these disorders and emerging on the other side with healthier mental and physical well-being.

References:
- Bulik, C. M., et al. (2016). Anorexia nervosa, bulimia nervosa, and binge-eating disorder. New England Journal of Medicine, 374(4), 354-361.
- Stice, E. (2002). Risk and maintenance factors for eating pathology: A meta-analytic review. Psychological Bulletin, 128(5), 825-848.
- National Eating Disorders Association. (2021). Health Consequences.
- Arcelus, J., et al. (2011). Mortality rates in patients with anorexia nervosa and other eating disorders: A meta-analysis of 36 studies. Archives of General Psychiatry, 68(7), 724-731.
- Fairburn, C. G., et al. (2015). Transdiagnostic cognitive-behavioral therapy for patients with eating disorders: A two-site trial with 60-week follow-up. American Journal of Psychiatry, 172(3), 274-281.
- Lock, J., et al. (2010). Randomized clinical trial comparing family-based treatment with adolescent-focused individual therapy for adolescents with anorexia nervosa. Archives of General Psychiatry, 67(10), 1025-1032.

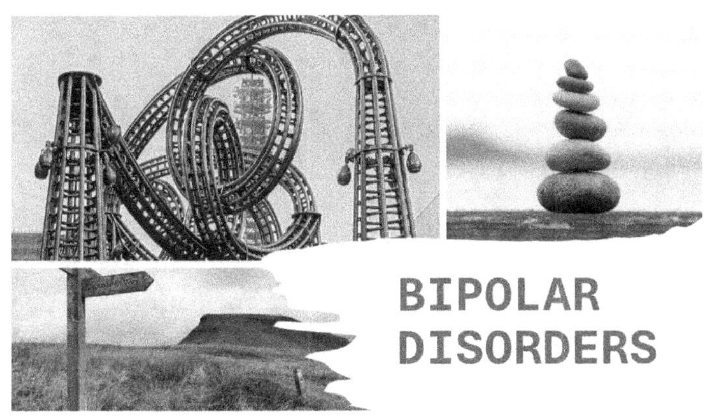

7. PSYCHOLOGICAL FACTS 7-11 - BIPOLAR DISORDERS

Understanding Bipolar Disorders: Symptoms, Types, and Effective Treatment Approaches

Introduction

Bipolar disorders represent a classification of mood disorders, distinctly marked by profound fluctuations in mood, energy, and activity levels. These shifts often oscillate between periods of intense elation or agitation (known as manic episodes) and bouts of deep depression, creating a polarized emotional landscape.

They are more than mere mood swings; bipolar disorders can drastically hinder an individual's daily activities, overall functioning, and indeed, their quality of life. These not only affect personal well-being but are prominent factors in shaping interpersonal relationships and career trajectories.

As conditions with a significant impact on emotional health, understanding these disorders necessitates a deep dive into their symptoms, diverse presentations (types), and the proven strategies for treating them. Symptoms associated with bipolar disorders are far from one-dimensional — they span the emotional, cognitive, and physiological domains and can vary significantly in severity and frequency.

These symptoms can be as dynamic as heightened energy and racing thoughts during a manic episode or as debilitating as feelings of despair and loss of interest during a depressive episode.

Bipolar disorders are also not a monolith — they encompass various types, each with unique symptom patterns and severities. These include Bipolar I, Bipolar II, Cyclothymic Disorder, and specified and unspecified bipolar and related disorders. Each presents a distinct combination of manic, hypomanic, and depressive episodes — a nuanced range that necessitates a detailed understanding to help tailor individual treatment plans.

In this comprehensive article, our investigation will extend into exploring the evidence-based treatment approaches for these multifaceted disorders. We will unpack a variety of treatments, which tend to leverage a multifaceted approach spanning pharmacological methods (such as mood stabilizers and antipsychotics), psychological therapy (like cognitive-behavioral therapy and family-focused therapy), and lifestyle modifications.

These interventions aim to manage symptoms, prevent relapses and equip individuals to lead balanced, fulfilling lives despite the disorder.

By demystifying bipolar disorders, shedding light on their intricacies, and underscoring the crucial need for strategic treatments, we hope this article will serve as a valuable resource — whether you are a caregiver, a professional, or someone navigating the journey of living with bipolar disorder.

Symptoms and Types of Bipolar Disorders

1. Bipolar I Disorder: Individuals experience manic episodes lasting at least one week. Some may also have depressive episodes.

2. Bipolar II Disorder: Individuals experience hypomanic episodes (less severe than full manic episodes) and major depressive episodes.

3. Cyclothymic Disorder: Individuals experience numerous periods of hypomanic and depressive symptoms over at least two years, but the symptoms are less severe and shorter in duration compared to full-blown episodes.

Symptoms of Manic Episodes

- Elevated mood and increased energy levels
- Decreased need for sleep
- Racing thoughts and rapid speech
- Impulsivity and risky behaviors
- Grandiosity and inflated self-esteem

Symptoms of Depressive Episodes

- Persistent sadness, hopelessness, and loss of interest in activities
- Changes in appetite and weight
- Fatigue and decreased energy
- Difficulty concentrating and making decisions
- Suicidal thoughts or behaviors

Effective Treatment Approaches for Bipolar Disorders

1. Medication: Mood stabilizers, such as lithium, are commonly prescribed to manage and stabilize mood symptoms. Other medications, such as antipsychotics and antidepressants, may be used in conjunction with mood stabilizers to address specific symptoms (National Institute of Mental Health, 2020).

2. Psychotherapy: Psychotherapy, particularly Cognitive Behavioral Therapy (CBT) and Interpersonal and Social Rhythm Therapy (IPSRT), can help individuals manage their symptoms, develop coping strategies, improve medication adherence, and enhance overall functioning (Miklowitz et al., 2020).

3. Psychoeducation: Learning about bipolar disorders, their symptoms, triggers, and treatment options can empower individuals to better understand and manage their condition. Psychoeducation also involves developing strategies for early recognition of warning signs.

4. Lifestyle Modifications: Establishing a regular sleep schedule, engaging in regular exercise, and maintaining a balanced diet can help stabilize mood and promote overall well-being.

5. Support Network: Building a strong support network of family, friends, and support groups can provide emotional support, encouragement, and understanding during challenging times.

6. Self-Care Practices: Engaging in self-care activities, such as relaxation techniques, stress management, and creative outlets, can help individuals manage stress, enhance self-esteem, and improve overall mental health.

Conclusion

Bipolar disorders represent an intricate class of mood disorders, distinctly marked by radical fluctuations in mood and levels of energy. These shifts range from deep and debilitating depressive lows to the extreme highs of mania.

It's essential that these disorders are not dismissed as mere mood swings but rather understood for their complexity and the significant impact they can have on an individual's day-to-day life. The effect on the individuals' quality of life can be profound, adversely impacting relationships, career progression, and overall life satisfaction.

Diverse treatments in an integrated approach have been shown to effectively tackle the multifaceted nature of bipolar disorders. This comprises a thoughtfully planned mix of medication, psychotherapy, psychoeducation, as well as the implementation of holistic strategies like lifestyle modifications, the cultivation of responsive support networks, and the habituation of self-care disciplines.

Medication plays a fundamental role in managing bipolar disorders. These can consist of mood stabilizers, antipsychotics, or antidepressants, generally prescribed in conjunction with one another to stabilize mood, curb manic symptoms, and treat depressive episodes.

Psychotherapy, another significant treatment factor, incorporates multiple behavioral therapy approaches. Cognitive behavioral therapy (CBT) helps individuals understand and manage their thought patterns, targeting distorted beliefs to alter behavior and effectively deal with life challenges. Furthermore, family-focused therapy may be used to strengthen the understanding and support within the family unit.

Psychoeducation, which promotes better understanding of the disorder, is crucial for effective self-management and can aid sufferers in recognizing early warning signals of mood shifts. It also increases compliance to medication plans and reduces the chance of relapses.

Moreover, lifestyle modifications like regular and sufficient sleep, balanced diet, and vigorous physical activity are strongly recommended to counteract the effects of bipolar disorders.

Furthermore, promoting solid and understanding support networks including family, friends and peer groups can protect against the isolating effects of the disease. Lastly, integrating regular self-care practices such as mindfulness, meditation, or yoga can help cultivate emotional stability and improve overall mental health.

In the journey of managing bipolar disorder, it is vital for those affected to seek and maintain close relationships with healthcare professionals, such as psychiatrists or psychologists. These professionals can aid in developing a tailored treatment scheme that aims to promote stability, manage symptoms, and enhance one's overall wellness.

A personalized approach allows room for adjustments according to the changing needs of individuals with bipolar disorder. This is a dynamic and ongoing process, necessitating constant engagement, regular evaluations, and revisions of the treatment plan as necessary.

Understanding this complex mental health condition and employing a comprehensive treatment approach can substantially enhance the quality of life for those living with bipolar disorder, allowing them to thrive and not just survive.

References:

- National Institute of Mental Health. (2020). Bipolar Disorder.
- Miklowitz, D. J., et al. (2020). Psychotherapy for bipolar disorder in adults: A review of the evidence. Focus, 18(1), 3-13.

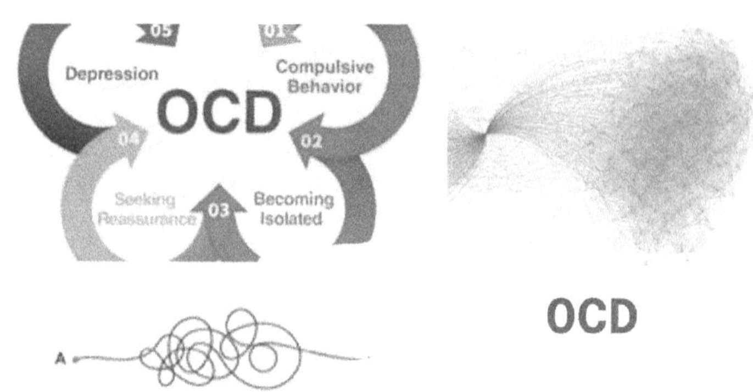

8. PSYCHOLOGICAL FACST 8-11 - OBSESSIVE-COMPULSIVE DISORDER (OCD)

Understanding Obsessive-Compulsive Disorders (OCD): Symptoms, Types, and Effective Treatment Approaches

Introduction

Obsessive-Compulsive Disorder (OCD) is a persistent mental health condition marked by uninvited, troubling thoughts known as obsessions and repetitive behaviors termed as compulsions. These obsessions and compulsions are conducted with the intent of suppressing the rising anxiety or distress associated with these intrusive thoughts. OCD is not just a series of habits or preferences, it's a severe condition with profound impacts on an individual's life and well-being.

OCD can dramatically interfere with everyday functioning and take an immense toll on the overall quality of life. The compulsive behaviors can become highly time-consuming, leading to debilitating levels of distress and anxiety. In more severe cases, OCD can lead to social isolation, lack of academic or occupational progress, and declining physical health due to the levels of stress and anxiety associated with the condition.

In unpacking OCD further, we understand that there are several types or subtypes of this disorder, including but not limited to: contamination obsessions with cleaning compulsions, symmetry obsessions with ordering compulsions, harm obsessions with checking compulsions, and obsessive thoughts without visible compulsions, also known as "Pure O."

Each of these subtypes carries its own distinct set of

symptoms and behaviors -- understanding these differences is of vital importance for the successful treatment and management of OCD. Grasping the spectrum of OCD nuances enables healthcare professionals to tailor interventions to meet the specific needs of an individual and adapt treatments accordingly over time.

Regarding treatments for OCD, conventional evidence-based methods include Cognitive Behavioral Therapy (CBT), exposure and response prevention (ERP), and medication. Cognitive Behavioral Therapy, specifically a subtype known as ERP, is considered the gold standard for treating OCD. It involves the individual facing their fears or obsessive thoughts and then refraining from conducting the associated compulsive behavior.

The goal of this therapy approach is to reduce the perceived threat of the obsessions and, therefore, lessen the need for compulsions.

Medication is also commonly used and can be especially effective when used in conjunction with therapy. These medications often serve to alter or control certain chemicals in the brain, such as serotonin, which can help to reduce the symptoms of OCD and provide some relief to affected individuals.

An increasingly popular adjunct to these conventional methodologies is the application of mindfulness and self-care practices. These can further help individuals manage their symptoms, enhance their distress tolerance, and reduce the overall impact of OCD on their lives.

Expanding the discourse around OCD not only promotes a greater understanding of the disorder but also sheds light on its intricacies and implications for treatment. In developing a comprehensive, nuanced understanding of OCD, we can ensure the timely and effective diagnosis and management of the condition, driving improved outcomes for those affected.

Symptoms and Types of OCD

1. Obsessions: Recurrent and intrusive thoughts, images, or urges that cause significant anxiety or distress. Common obsessions include contamination fears, fears of harming oneself or others, and perfectionism.

2. Compulsions: Repetitive behaviors or mental acts performed in response to obsessions, with the aim of reducing anxiety or preventing a feared event. Examples include excessive handwashing, checking behaviors, and mental rituals.

3. Types of OCD: OCD can manifest in various subtypes, including contamination OCD, symmetry and ordering OCD, hoarding OCD, and intrusive thoughts OCD, among others.

Effective Treatment Approaches for OCD

1. Cognitive Behavioral Therapy (CBT): CBT, specifically Exposure and Response Prevention (ERP), is the gold standard treatment for OCD. ERP involves gradual and systematic exposure to feared situations or thoughts, without engaging in the associated compulsions. This process helps individuals learn to tolerate anxiety and break the cycle of obsessions and compulsions (Abramowitz et al., 2019).

2. Medication: Selective Serotonin Reuptake Inhibitors (SSRIs), such as fluoxetine and sertraline, are often prescribed as a first-line medication treatment for OCD. These medications help regulate serotonin levels in the brain and can reduce OCD symptoms (National Institute of Mental Health, 2019).

3. Mindfulness-Based Therapies: Mindfulness-based approaches, such as Mindfulness-Based Cognitive Therapy (MBCT) and Acceptance and Commitment Therapy (ACT), can help individuals develop acceptance and non-judgmental awareness of their obsessions and compulsions. These therapies promote psychological flexibility and a more compassionate approach to

one's thoughts and emotions (Hwang et al., 2019).

4. Support Groups: Participating in support groups, such as those offered by the International OCD Foundation, can provide individuals with a sense of community, understanding, and shared experiences. Support groups also offer a platform for individuals to learn from each other and exchange coping strategies.

5. Family Involvement: Involving family members in treatment can enhance understanding, support, and communication. Family therapy can address family dynamics, educate loved ones about OCD, and help them provide appropriate support.

Conclusion

Obsessive-Compulsive Disorder (OCD) is indeed a formidable mental health issue, primarily distinguished by its persistent and intrusive thoughts as well as compulsive behaviors that noticeably interfere with a person's everyday life.

This disorder, often misunderstood, requires greater awareness and understanding as it is more complex than simple habitual routines or preferences for orderliness, and thus necessitates professional attention for its management.

Various evidence-based treatment approaches have consistently shown efficacy in dealing with OCD. Among these, Cognitive Behavioral Therapy (CBT) coupled with Exposure and Response Prevention (ERP) is a standout choice.

This method encourages individuals to face their fears and learn healthier coping mechanisms, instead of resorting to compulsive behaviors to alleviate their anxiety. CBT is a structured, time-limited practice that directly targets OCD symptoms and has received robust support from numerous studies.

Medication is another critical component of treatment — many individuals find a significant symptom reduction with specifically prescribed Selective Serotonin Reuptake Inhibitors (SSRIs) or other psychiatric medications. This biochemical approach, potentially combined with psychotherapy, often brings about significant relief from the crippling effects of OCD.

Furthermore, mindfulness-based therapies are gaining traction. These therapies focus on teaching individuals to stay present and respond wisely to intrusive thoughts and urges. Techniques such as mindful breathing, progressive muscle relaxation, and meditation help those with OCD reduce the distress associated with their symptoms and cultivate a more gentle and accepting attitude towards their experience.

Equally important are supportive environments, such as OCD support groups. Here, individuals can connect with others who share similar experiences, empowering them to discuss their challenges, learn from others, obtain validation, and find a sense of belonging.

Family involvement in the treatment process is another critical factor. Relatives need to understand the nature of OCD and be equipped to provide the right balance of empathy and encouragement needed for their loved ones to continue their progress.

In summary, it is crucial for individuals with OCD to reach out for professional assistance and fully engage in a comprehensive, multi-faceted treatment plan. This engagement not only aids in managing the challenging symptoms but also significantly reduces the distress associated with OCD, fostering an enhanced sense of control, and ultimately, an improved quality of life.

References:
- Abramowitz, J. S., et al. (2019). The psychological treatment of obsessive-compulsive disorder. Canadian Journal of Psychiatry, 64(6), 406-413.

- National Institute of Mental Health. (2019). Obsessive-Compulsive Disorder.

- Hwang, I., et al. (2019). Mindfulness-based interventions for obsessive-compulsive disorder: A systematic review and meta-analysis. International Journal of Environmental Research and Public

Health, 16(21), 4116.

- International OCD Foundation. (n.d.). OCD Support Groups. Retrieved from https://iocdf.org/supportgroups/

51

9. PSYCHOLOGICAL FACTS 9-11 – SCHIZOPHRENIA

Understanding Schizophrenia: Symptoms, Types, and Effective Treatment Approaches

Introduction

Schizophrenia is an intricate and often misconstrued mental health condition, impacting a multitude of crucial cognitive functions within an individual. This influences how an individual conceptualizes reality, processes emotions, and interacts with their environment, creating significant hurdles in day-to-day functioning and well-being. The effects of schizophrenia are profound, interfering not just with occupational and interpersonal relationships but with the ability to engage in the most mundane activities.

This article's main thrust is to delve deeply into the varying aspects of this mental disorder. It is designed to provide a comprehensive overview of the characteristic symptomatology, the different subtypes, as well as the most successful intervention strategies currently employed in the mental health field to manage and treat schizophrenia.

We are going to delve headfirst into the myriad symptoms commonly associated with schizophrenia—these can range from debilitating delusions to complex hallucinations, disoriented thinking to emotional deregulation. By gaining a deep understanding of these manifestations, we can begin to grasp the inherent difficulties experienced by those diagnosed with schizophrenia.

Further on, we will venture into the territory of different schizophrenia types or classifications. This is crucial, as recognizing the subtype can drastically influence the course of treatment and management, ensuring a tailored and person-centric approach to care.

Lastly, but just as importantly, we're going to explore the current prominent treatment approaches utilized in managing schizophrenia. From psychotherapeutic interventions to psychopharmacology and community-focused support mechanisms, we hope to underline the multitude of ways available to effectively address, manage, and hopefully, significantly diminish the substantial impact of schizophrenia on affected individuals' lives.

In essence, this article aims to increase understanding of schizophrenia, making it less of an enigmatic, misunderstood entity and more of a comprehensible, manageably complex condition. Our hope is to empower readers with knowledge, whether they are individuals facing schizophrenia, their loved ones, or those simply seeking to better understand this intricate mental health disorder.

Symptoms and Types of Schizophrenia

1. Positive Symptoms: These symptoms involve an excess or distortion of normal functions. They include hallucinations (seeing or hearing things that aren't there), delusions (strongly held false beliefs), and disorganized speech or behavior.

2. Negative Symptoms: These symptoms reflect a loss or reduction of normal functions. They include a lack of motivation or pleasure in activities, reduced emotional expression, and difficulties with speech and social interactions.

3. Types of Schizophrenia: There are different types of schizophrenia, including paranoid, disorganized, catatonic, undifferentiated, and residual, each with its own characteristic symptoms.

Effective Treatment Approaches for Schizophrenia

1. Medication: Antipsychotic medications, prescribed by a psychiatrist, are commonly used to manage schizophrenia symptoms. These medications help regulate brain chemicals to reduce hallucinations, delusions, and other symptoms.

2. Psychotherapy: Different types of therapy, such as Cognitive Behavioral Therapy (CBT) and supportive therapy, can help individuals better understand and manage their symptoms, improve coping skills, and enhance overall functioning.

3. Psychosocial Interventions: Psychosocial interventions, including social skills training and vocational rehabilitation, can assist individuals in developing practical skills, improving relationships, and increasing independence in daily life.

4. Family Support and Education: Involving family members in treatment can provide support, enhance understanding, and improve communication. Family education programs can help loved ones learn about the illness, develop coping strategies, and create a supportive environment.

5. Support Groups: Participating in support groups, either in-person or online, can provide individuals with schizophrenia a sense of community, understanding, and the opportunity to share experiences and coping strategies.

Conclusion

Schizophrenia manifests as an intricate and multifaceted mental health disorder, possessing the significant potential to create profound changes in an individual's life trajectory. This impactful nature of the disorder underpins the crucial importance of comprehensive, targeted treatment strategies that can effectively counteract its wide-ranging symptoms.

Instrumental in the successful treatment of schizophrenia is a strategic combination of various methodologies, each selected to address specific aspects of the condition. Among these supportive treatments is the judicious administration of medication, which plays a crucial role in mitigating the severity of symptoms, thus optimizing therapeutic outcomes.

Psychotherapy, too, is a highly beneficial tool, enabling individuals to understand their condition better, manage their symptoms more effectively, and foster resilience against the psychological stresses often accompanying schizophrenia.

Moreover, an equally integral part of this multifaceted approach to treatment encompasses psychosocial interventions. They are particularly effective in readying the individuals to reintegrate into society, improving their interpersonal and communication skills, and equipping them with the necessary coping mechanisms to navigate daily life. By bolstering these skills, such interventions also pave the way for individuals with schizophrenia to regain control of their lives and foster their ability to function independently.

The robust involvement of family is another pivotal aspect of a comprehensive approach to managing schizophrenia. Unconditional family support and education can drastically enhance an individual's capacity to adapt to the disorder. It can help construct a nurturing and understanding environment essential for recovery, allowing them to positively engage with their therapy.

This kind of commitment can also empower family members, giving them the knowledge to be able to provide effective support and manage crises if they arise, ensuring the individual's safety and general welfare.

Participation in support groups is another powerful resource for individuals with schizophrenia. It offers them the unique opportunity to connect with others who share similar experiences, promoting a sense of community, mutual empathy, and solidarity that can markedly boost their spirits and motivation towards recovery.

Central to the management and treatment of schizophrenia, however, is the person's proactive role in their journey towards health. Working closely with healthcare professionals enables them to actively participate in their treatment process, fostering a sense of control and optimism that can greatly impact their overall progress. The consistent adherence to their prescribed treatment plan is fundamental as it ensures they are getting the optimal benefits from their therapeutic regimen.

It rises to prominence that having a robust support system is integral for individuals battling schizophrenia. A nurturing network of friends, family, and professionals can provide the emotional, practical, and psychological support needed to successfully manage their symptoms. This kind of invaluable support also helps them maintain a positive outlook, empowering them to steadily improve their overall well-being and increase their chances of leading fulfilling, independent lives.

Overall, effectively managing schizophrenia involves a concerted, comprehensive approach that involves multiple different strategies and resources, the individuals' active involvement, and the unwavering support of family, friends, and healthcare professionals. This dynamic and interactive approach ensures that individuals not only learn to cope with their condition but actively strive towards a future rich in promise and fulfillment.

References:

- National Institute of Mental Health. (2020). Schizophrenia.
- American Psychiatric Association. (2013). Diagnostic and Statistical Manual of Mental Disorders
(5th ed.). Arlington, VA: American Psychiatric Publishing.
- Dixon, L. B., et al. (2010). The Efficacy of Psychosocial Interventions for Adults With Schizophrenia: A Meta-analysis of Randomized Controlled Trials. American Journal of Psychiatry,
167(11), 1247–1258.
- Substance Abuse and Mental Health Services Administration. (2014). Schizophrenia Treatment. Treatment Improvement Protocol (TIP) Series, No. 58. Rockville, MD: Substance Abuse and Mental Health Services Administration.

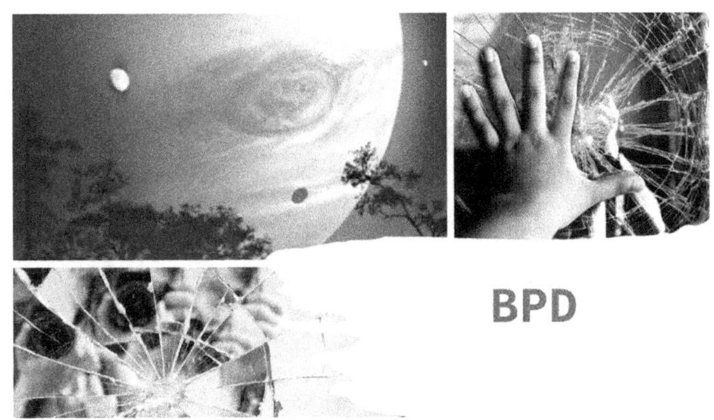

10. PSYCHOLOGICAL FACTS 10-11 - BORDERLINE PERSONALITY DISORDER (BPD)

Understanding Borderline Personality Disorder (BPD):Symptoms, Types, and Effective Treatment Approaches

Introduction

Borderline Personality Disorder (BPD), a complex and often misunderstood mental health disorder, is primarily distinguished by its manifestations of volatile emotions, tumultuous relationships, and impulsive actions. These chief characteristics can lead to profound complications, often transforming routine life into a series of formidable challenges. In this comprehensive discourse, we aim to journey deeper into the terrain of BPD by dissecting its core components, wherein we will delve into its symptoms, understand its various types, and shed light on effective treatment protocols.

BPD is particularly potent in its ability to manipulate a person's emotional state, leading to intensely charged feelings that can fluctuate dramatically and unpredictably. These emotional rollercoasters present a profound impact on the individual's interactions with others, rooting BPD as one of the key causes of unstable interpersonal relationships. The disorder is also inseparable from certain impulsive behaviors that can disrupt a person's daily life, causing potentially harmful consequences.

However, living with BPD is not an insurmountable hurdle. Through a detailed understanding of its symptoms and subtypes, the quest towards effective management becomes more attainable. Accordingly, we will dissect the various symptoms that hallmark BPD, aiming to provide a comprehensive view of how this disorder presents itself. Relying on this understanding, we will also present the recognized types or classifications of BPD, as recognizing the specific subtype can often provide valuable guidance for treatment strategies.

No account of BPD is complete without exploring the various therapeutic approaches designed to tackle the symptoms and effects of the disorder. Understanding these interventions is fundamental, as it equips both individuals with BPD and their loved ones with the knowledge needed to navigate their journey with the disorder. Therefore, in parallel with our exploration of symptoms and types, we will also illuminate these treatment approaches, providing a balanced view of the benefits and limitations of each.

Circling back to our initial focus, this detailed exploration of Borderline Personality Disorder aims at equipping the reader with an enhanced understanding of the disorder. This may aid in diminishing the stigma associated with BPD and empowering those affected to better understand their condition, subsequently encouraging more effective participation in therapeutic avenues and fostering hope for stability and improved daily living.

Symptoms and Types of Borderline Personality Disorder

1. Emotional Instability: Individuals with BPD often experience intense and rapidly shifting emotions, including anger, sadness, and anxiety. These emotions can be difficult to manage and may lead to impulsive or self-destructive behaviors.

2. Unstable Relationships: People with BPD may struggle with maintaining stable and healthy relationships due to fears of abandonment, idealization, and devaluation of others.

3. Impulsive Behaviors: Individuals with BPD may engage in impulsive actions such as reckless spending, substance abuse, self-harm, and risky sexual behaviors.

4. Identity Disturbance: People with BPD may struggle with a sense of self, feeling uncertain about their values, goals, and identity.

Effective Treatment Approaches for Borderline Personality Disorder

1. Dialectical Behavior Therapy (DBT): DBT is a specific type of therapy designed for individuals with BPD. It focuses on teaching skills to manage emotions, improve interpersonal relationships, and develop coping strategies. DBT incorporates individual therapy, group skills training, phone coaching, and therapist consultation to provide comprehensive support (Linehan, 2015).

2. Medication: Medication may be prescribed to address specific symptoms related to depression, anxiety, or mood stabilization. However, medication is typically used in conjunction with therapy rather than as the sole treatment for BPD.

3. Psychoeducation: Learning about BPD can help individuals understand their symptoms and develop strategies for managing them. Psychoeducation can also involve teaching loved ones about the disorder to improve support and communication.

4. Supportive Therapy: Supportive therapy provides a safe and empathetic space for individuals with BPD to express their feelings, gain insights, and receive validation. The therapist offers support and guidance throughout the treatment process.

5. Group Therapy: Participating in group therapy with others who have BPD can provide a sense of belonging, reduce feelings of isolation, and offer opportunities for practicing interpersonal skills and receiving support from peers.

6. Self-care and Healthy Lifestyle: Engaging in self-care activities, practicing relaxation techniques, maintaining a balanced diet, exercising regularly, and getting enough sleep can contribute to overall well-being and mood stability.

Conclusion

Borderline Personality Disorder (BPD) stands as a significant mental health malady, distinguished by its unique portrayal of severe emotional fluctuations, unsteady relationships, and erratic actions that make navigating life's waters particularly challenging for those diagnosed with this condition.

People with BPD often oscillate between feelings of intense love and hate, struggle with fear of abandonment, and can engage in self-destructive actions due to their impulsive tendencies. Each of these compounding factors underlines the need for an effective, multifaceted treatment plan that addresses the complexities of this disorder.

Two key therapeutic approaches that have demonstrated efficacy in managing BPD-related symptoms include Dialectical Behavior Therapy (DBT) and medication management. DBT, in particular, equips patients with coping and social skills necessary to handle their intense emotions, manage their interpersonal relationships, and mitigate self-destructive behaviors.

It's a form of cognitive-behavioral therapy that emphasizes the balance between acceptance and change, providing tools for mindfulness, emotional regulation, distress tolerance, and interpersonal effectiveness. The feasibility of these techniques extends their use beyond therapy sessions, allowing individuals to independently manage crises and reduce their disruptive impulsivity.

On the other hand, medication administration serves as a beneficial approach, especially when BPD symptoms coexist with other mental health problems like anxiety disorder or depression. Medication assists in lowering emotional instability, reducing impulsivity, and tempering any accompanying mental health issues, thereby creating a conducive environment for other forms of therapy to flourish.

An often underutilized, yet essential aspect of BPD treatment, is psychoeducation. Learning about BPD and understanding its intricacies fosters transparency between patients and healthcare professionals, breaks down barriers of stigma, and promotes personal ownership over their recovery journey. Psychoeducation empowers patients by providing crucial knowledge about their mental health condition, thereby equipping them with the necessary awareness to recognize when their behaviors are driven by BPD and providing tools to better manage their symptoms.

Moreover, the efficacy of supportive therapy and group therapy should not be discounted. The nurturing atmosphere of supportive therapy can provide emotional resilience and stability to individuals, while group therapy serves as a platform for individuals to connect with others who share similar experiences, creating a sense of communal understanding and shared growth.

Emphasizing the importance of self-care practices acts as the capstone to a comprehensive BPD treatment plan. Regular physical exercise, proper nutrition, sufficient sleep, and mindfulness practices can significantly supplement therapeutic interventions, helping individuals manage their symptoms and avoid potential triggers.

In managing BPD, the interplay of professional help, therapeutic treatments, and a supportive network plays a pivotal role. The combination of these elements aids in symptom management, ensuring steady improvement in the overall well-being of those with BPD.

These interventions can support individuals diagnosed with BPD in their journey towards wellness, enabling them to lead more fruitful, fulfilling lives, and highlighting the possibility of recovery with the right resources and treatment approaches.

References:

- Linehan, M. M. (2015). DBT Skills Training Manual (2nd ed.). New York, NY: The Guilford Press.

- National Institute of Mental Health. (2020). Borderline Personality Disorder.

- American Psychiatric Association. (2013). Diagnostic and Statistical Manual of Mental Disorders (5th ed.). Arlington, VA: American Psychiatric Publishing.

- Gunderson, J. G. (2011). Borderline Personality Disorder: Ontogeny of a Diagnosis. American Journal of Psychiatry, 168(1), 3–6.

11. PSYCHOLOGICAL FACTS 11-11 - CELEBRITIES SHARING THEIR PERSONAL MENTAL HEALTH JOURNEYS."

Celebrities Revolutionizing Mental Health Narratives:Inspiring Stories of Hope and Resilience

Introduction

R ecent decades have experienced a significant shift in our cultural and societal norms, primarily driven by an increasing recognition of the critical importance of mental health and its impact on holistic well-being. A prominent force behind this cultural metamorphosis is popular media, traditionally casting a long shadow over societal attitudes and norms.

As influential figures in these realms, celebrities have uniquely leveraged their platforms, sparking intriguing and paramount dialogues about mental health issues. Sharing their deeply personal journeys, celebrities from diverse backgrounds and industries have stepped into the limelight, elucidating conditions that have often been shrouded in misunderstanding or stigma, such as anxiety, depression, PTSD, among others.

In a society where fame and fortune often mask the struggles of celebrities, these figures' candid admissions have revolutionized narratives surrounding mental health. Musicians, actors, athletes, and more have garnished their fame with evocative tales of their respective encounters with mental health conditions, revealing an often-hidden human side behind the glitz and glamor.

Their stories inspire hope, bolster resilience, and further reveal the commonality of these struggles, asserting that nobody, regardless of status or reputation, is immune to mental health concerns.

Each brave confession brings with it the power to lift stigma, offering a refreshing, unapologetic account on a global platform. These admissions resonate with millions of fans worldwide, helping to normalize conversations around mental health and encouraging individuals to seek assistance when needed.

Moreover, by articulating their experiences with conditions such as anxiety, depression, and PTSD, these celebrities have made strides in empowering people with similar struggles to feel seen and understood. Their courage prompts the understanding that mental health conditions do not signify weakness or flaws but are a part of the collective human experience that can be managed with appropriate care.

Their openness and vulnerability have played a pivotal role in reducing the stigma surrounding mental health, while inspiring countless individuals to seek help and support. This article explores how celebrities sharing their experiences have turned the spotlight on mental health, transforming it into a viral hot topic.

a. Breaking the Silence

Celebrities hold immense influence over society, and when they use their platforms to discuss their mental health struggles, it breaks down barriers and encourages open conversations. By revealing their vulnerabilities, they humanize mental health conditions and demonstrate that anyone can be affected, regardless of fame or success. Their courage to share personal stories has sparked a new era of empathy and understanding, fostering a safe space for individuals to seek help.

b. Challenging Stigma and Stereotypes

Historically, mental health has carried a heavy burden of stigma and misconceptions. However, by openly discussing their struggles, celebrities have played a crucial role in challenging these stereotypes. They have brought attention to the fact that mental health conditions are not a sign of weakness, but rather a part of the human experience. Through their stories, they have shattered the illusion of perfection and presented mental health as a universal concern that deserves compassion and support.

c. Inspiring Hope and Resilience

The journeys of celebrities battling mental health conditions provide inspiration and hope to millions of people who may be experiencing similar challenges. By sharing their stories of recovery and resilience, these celebrities showcase that there is light at the end of the tunnel. Their narratives demonstrate that seeking help, therapy, and adopting healthy coping mechanisms can lead to a fulfilling and meaningful life.

This message of hope resonates with individuals who may have felt isolated, offering them the belief that they too can overcome their struggles.

d. Amplifying Awareness and Advocacy

Celebrities possess a unique ability to capture public attention, and when they speak out about mental health, it amplifies awareness on a global scale. Their influence extends beyond their immediate fan base, reaching a broader audience and sparking conversations in various media outlets.

This increased awareness not only encourages individuals to seek help but also drives societal change by advocating for better mental health resources, policies, and support systems.

e. The Power of Social Media

Social media platforms have become powerful tools for celebrities to share their mental health journeys directly with their followers. Platforms like Instagram, Twitter, and YouTube allow for authentic and unfiltered narratives, enabling celebrities to connect with their fans on a personal level. These platforms also provide a safe space for individuals to engage in discussions, share their own experiences, and find solace in a supportive community.

Conclusion

The emergence of stars who bravely reveal their mental health struggles has instigated a world-wide movement, transforming the perception and conversation around mental health into a global phenomenon that cannot be ignored. These celebrities, who voluntarily step out of the shadows into the spotlight of vulnerability, have boldly confronted the societal stigma and misconceptions regarding mental health, thereby becoming agents of significant positive change.

By openly discussing their experiences, they are driving forth a new wave of dialogue and discourse about mental health, making it a household conversation instead of a hushed taboo. Such bold acts feed into a global network of shared experiences, provoking a collective sense of empathy and understanding that emphasizes the very human nature of mental health struggles.

Their unfaltering determination and persistence in the face of adversity inspire hope in those who are in similar predicaments, encouraging them to communicate their struggles and seek professional help. Their actions are redrawing the societal contours concerning mental health, forging a more inclusive narrative that fosters acceptance and eschews prejudice.

As the reach of the stories shared by these celebrities expands, penetrating even remote corners of the world, we envision a future with amplified compassion and understanding towards those grappling with mental health issues. A future where humanity collectively acknowledges the reality of mental health challenges, and strives to create supportive environments for those affected.

These celebrities' voices echo in the silence, turning the tide through the powerful media of visibility and frank discourse - they have taken their personal fights and transformed them into a beacon of hope for millions who are silently battling mental health issues. Their courage and candidness have crafted a new path that illuminates the darkness of silence and stigma.

Let us not just celebrate these brave individuals for their talents and fame, but more vitally, for their pivotal role in driving a wave of transformation, by using their platforms to instigate ground-breaking conversations around mental health. They provide a lifeline and a voice for those who, in their silence, often feel drowned in the grand scheme of society.

These celebrities are indeed torchbearers in this revolution to banish the shadows of mental health stigma. Despite the disheartening stories of struggle that they share, it is inspiring to see how they transform their battles into a stepping stone to drive a global initiative. It's this action, this catalyst for change, that truly shows us a future where openness, understanding, and support of mental health become interwoven into the fabric of our societies.